Contents

Some words are printed in bold, **like this**. You can find out what they mean by looking in the glossary.

WORLD IN PERIL

MOUNTAINS
UNDER THREAT

PAUL MASON

www.heinemannlibrary.co.uk

Visit our website to find out more information about Heinemann Library books.

To order:

☎ Phone +44 (0) 1865 888066

▤ Fax +44 (0) 1865 314091

▥ Visit www.heinemannlibrary.co.uk

Edited by Louise Galpine and Rachel Howells
Designed by Richard Parker and Manhattan Design
Picture research by Hannah Taylor and Rebecca Sodergren
Production by Alison Parsons
Originated by Dot Gradations Ltd.
Printed in China by Leo Paper Products Ltd.

ISBN 978 0 431020 61 7 (hardback)
13 12 11 10 09
10 9 8 7 6 5 4 3 2 1

British Library Cataloguing in Publication Data
Mason, Paul
Mountains under threat. – (World in peril)
577.5'3

A full catalogue record for this book is available from the British Library.

Acknowledgements

We would like to thank the following for permission to reproduce photographs: Corbis pp. **13** (Ecoscene; Ian Harwood), **15** (Lester Lefkowitz), **17** (Galen Rowell); Gamma p. **16** (Pierre-Yves GINET / RAPHO); Getty Images pp. **6** (Time & Life Pictures/ Alfred Eisenstaedt), **14** (James Randklev), **26** (Paula Bronstein); Jupiter Images p. **11** (Robert Harding/ Hans Peter Merten); Panos pp. **19** (Chris de Bode); **25** (Polaris/ Yannis Kontos); Photolibrary pp. **4** (Mike Norton), **7** (Pixland), **9** (OSF/ Mary Plage), **10** (Jon Arnold), **12** (Imagesource), **22** (Robert Winslow), **24** (Jacob Halaska), **27** (Hemis/ Pierre Jacques); Rex Features pp. **20** and **21** (Bjorn Lux/ Frank Wche), **23** (SIPA Press); Still Pictures p. **18** (Biosphoto / Gunther Michel); Topham Picturepoint p. **8**.

Cover photograph of small aeroplane flying over a glacier in Wrangell St. Elias National Park, Alaska, reproduced with permission of Corbis (Frans Lanting).

We would like to thank Michael Mastrandrea for his invaluable help in the preparation of this book.

Every effort has been made to contact copyright holders of material reproduced in this book. Any omissions will be rectified in subsequent printings if notice is given to the publishers.

All the Internet addresses (URLs) given in this book were valid at the time of going to press. However, due to the dynamic nature of the Internet, some addresses may have changed, or sites may have changed or ceased to exist since publication. While the author and Publishers regret any inconvenience this may cause readers, no responsibility for any such changes can be accepted by either the author or the Publishers.

Aren't mountains indestructible?

Mountains are among our oldest landscapes. Can you imagine how long the Rocky Mountains have existed? They have stood for more than 65 million years. These huge, towering rocks seem indestructible. In fact, the mountain **environment** is delicate and easily damaged.

The mountain environment is **unique**. Mountains are home to many different **habitats**. The valleys are often filled with rushing rivers, fed by rainfall and melting snow from the upper slopes. The lower slopes can be warm and damp, and thick with trees and other plants. Higher up it is often cold and dry, and the mountainside may be nothing but bare stone and ice.

Nowhere other than in the mountains are so many different habitats packed into such a small space. Many of the animals that live on mountains are specially **adapted** to these conditions.

Today, humans are putting the world's mountains under threat. We have driven many animals from their homes. Worse, we have caused changes to the **climate** that mean the unique mountain environment is under threat.

How are mountain towns changing?

This photograph shows a town clinging to a steep, mountainous slope in Italy, in 1947. In the past, mountain **settlements** such as this were almost always small. There was not much space on the **valley floor** for houses and farmland. This meant that the settlements could never grow beyond a certain size. People living in the mountains had a small impact on the surrounding **environment**.

How much bigger does the same town look in this photograph, taken 60 years later? Many mountain towns have grown very quickly in recent years. This is causing big problems. **Pollution** from the towns gets into the water, affecting fish and plants. The towns produce far more waste than ever before. Rubbish is blown by the wind to the farthest corners of the mountains.

What would it be like to wake up in a lonely tent here? These **mountaineers** are on Everest in 1953. Mountaineering expeditions like this became popular during the 1800s. People wanted to visit the wild countryside. A few took up the challenge of climbing to the top of the highest mountain **peaks**.

Unfortunately, mountaineers soon began to spoil the wild beauty that had brought them to the mountains in the first place.

This is just some of the rubbish that surrounds Everest Base Camp today. Many popular mountaineering sites now look more like rubbish tips than beauty spots. Over the years, climbers have left behind old tents, ropes, food, rubbish, and even piles of human waste. Can you imagine the smell? The problem has become so bad that some expeditions now go to Everest simply to clean, rather than to climb.

What would it be like to carry your shopping bags by yak, as is often done in Nepal? It used to take everyone a long time to get around in the mountains. There were few roads, and they were often closed by snow in winter. Whole villages would be cut off until the snow melted in spring. As a result, not many people from outside visited mountain areas.

This road makes the journey into the Austrian Alps far quicker than before. Today, new roads have made it much easier to get into the mountains. However, the mountains are being changed as a result of the extra traffic. The roads are dangerous for animals, and many are killed trying to cross. The roads bring millions of visitors, plus **logging** and other **industries** that affect the **environment**. All the extra vehicles release air **pollution**.

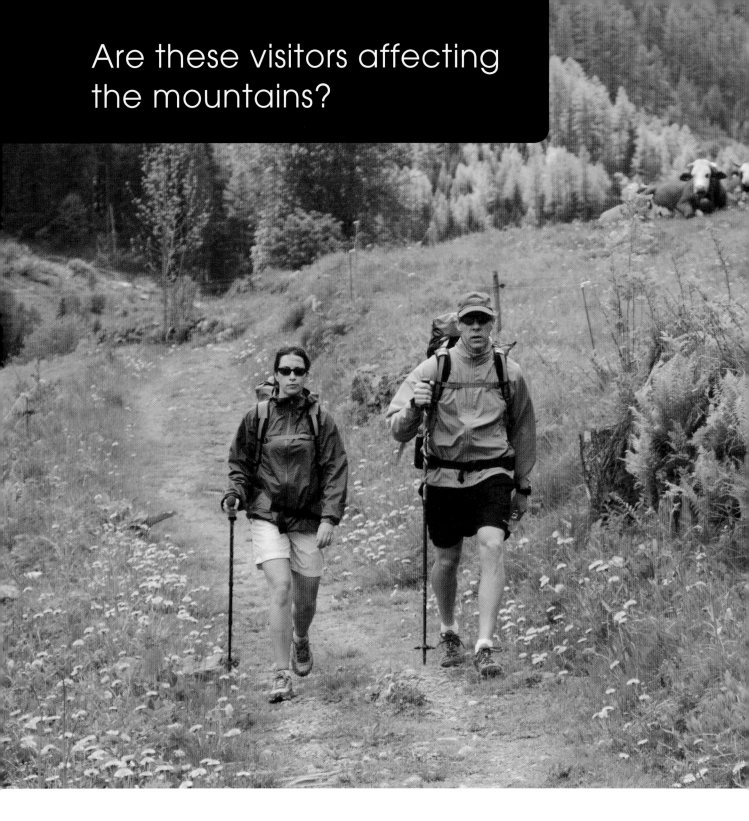

Are these visitors affecting the mountains?

Have you ever thought about the damage your steps might do? In the mountains, people need to be careful where they tread. The mountain **environment** is delicate. The mountain soil is very thin, and grasses and flowers can easily be damaged. Once plants have worn away, they can take years to recover. This is why hikers, like these people in the French Alps, are always encouraged to stick to the marked paths.

The snow on this ski slope is melting at the end of the winter.
During the ski season, machines were used to make **pistes**.
Pistes are the snowy routes down the mountain used by skiers and
snowboarders. The piste-making machines have ripped up the grass
and flowers beneath the snow. Now the snow is melting, the slopes
are left bare and brown. When it rains, the soil washes down the
slope. After this, plants will find it hard to grow here.

Who drinks the mountain water?

What do you think allows these beautiful flowers to grow? The answer is water. After rain, water runs down the mountain slopes in fast-flowing streams. On the **valley floor** these become rivers. The rivers and streams allow plants, animals, and humans to survive in the mountains. As a result, mountain valleys are home to lots of different plants and animals. Some of them are very **rare**, and are only found in a few valleys.

Today, we use huge amounts of water at home, on farms, and for **industry**. As a result, many mountain rivers have been **dammed**. A giant lake like this one behind the Hoover Dam in the United States builds up. The stored water can then be piped wherever it is needed. Other dams are built for **hydroelectric** schemes. The result is the same: the plants, animals, and people that lived in the valley lose their homes.

Where did all the trees go?

Trees do not grow high up in the mountains because it is too cold. Lower down, forests can be so thick that it is dark inside them even on the brightest day.

Mountain people have always used wood from the forests for heating and cooking. When few people lived in the mountains, few trees were chopped down. A new tree grew for every one that had been chopped down, so the forests were unaffected.

How did this slope come to lose its trees? Today, more people live in the mountains than ever before. More trees are being chopped down for fuel. Some slopes are now completely bare of trees. This is called **deforestation**.

Tree roots hold the soil in place on the slope. Without the roots, the soil is washed away by rainfall. Once the soil is gone, nothing can be grown on the bare mountainside.

What is the best way to cook a mountain dinner?

What would it be like to do all your cooking on a wood fire? This cooking fire in Nepal looks warm and welcoming from the outside, in the cold mountain air. But imagine how smoky it gets inside!

The problem with making a fire like this is that it uses a lot of wood. Many trees have to be cut down to provide a year's firewood. The smoke from the fire also fills the room, making it hard to breathe.

These mountain homes are in a part of Nepal that suffers from **deforestation**. Recently, though, **environmental** charities have been handing out solar cookers in some villages. This family won theirs after coming third in a solar-cooker cookery competition!

The sunlight is strong high up in the mountains. Solar power can provide energy for cooking, heat, and light. This means fewer trees have to be cut down.

What caused the glaciers to disappear?

This photograph of the Tour **glacier**, high above the French town of Chamonix, was taken in 1998. The glacier had taken thousands of years to form. As new snow fell at the top of the valley, old snow was forced downwards. Eventually, the old snow was squeezed down so hard, it turned into ice. The icy glacier finally covered the mountains and spilled downwards.

This is the same glacier nine years later. It has melted because Earth's average temperature is slowly rising. This **global warming** is mainly caused by human **pollution**, especially pollution from cars and **industry**. How long before the glacier disappears completely?

For hundreds of years, the tops of many mountains have been held together by solid ice. This ice has now started to melt. The mountaintops are falling apart.

Could avalanche disasters be avoided?

Can you imagine being in the way of an **avalanche** like this one in Colorado, USA? Avalanches happen when it is warm enough to melt snow during the day. At night, the melted snow freezes into ice. If lots of new snow then falls, it sometimes slides off the icy surface, causing an avalanche.

Rising temperatures caused by **global warming** mean that warm, snow-melting days are more common, especially in springtime.

This photograph shows the effects of an avalanche that hit the French village of Montroc in 1999. Twelve people were killed and seventeen buildings destroyed. Even though the area had suffered from avalanches before, new houses had been built in Montroc.

The demand for **building land** in the mountains grows all the time, as the population of mountain areas increases. Combined with the increasing number of avalanches, this may lead to disaster.

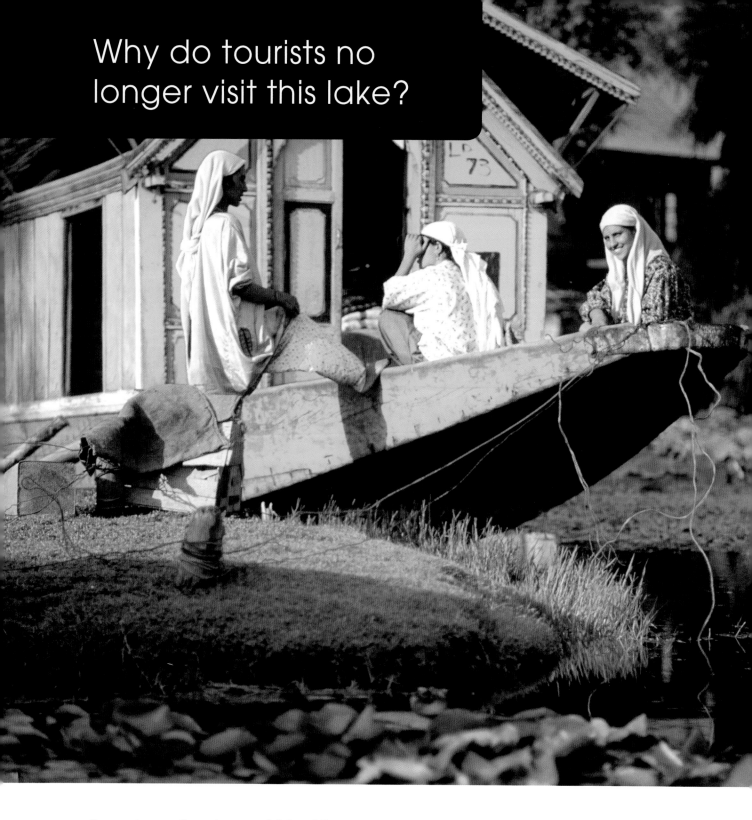

Why do tourists no longer visit this lake?

Imagine what it would be like to live on a houseboat, like these women in Kashmir, India. For hundreds of years, the lakes of Kashmir have been a popular place for travellers to visit. The houseboats provide tourists with somewhere to stay.

Kashmir is divided between China, India, and Pakistan. But these countries cannot agree on who owns Kashmir. This means the peace is often broken by one more human effect on the mountains – war.

Mountains often form the **border** between countries. They make a natural barrier. If countries disagree on exactly where the border should be, problems can develop. This Pakistani soldier is looking across towards the Indian-controlled part of Kashmir.

Pakistan and India have fought three wars over Kashmir. Today, most governments ask their **citizens** not to visit Kashmir because it is so dangerous.

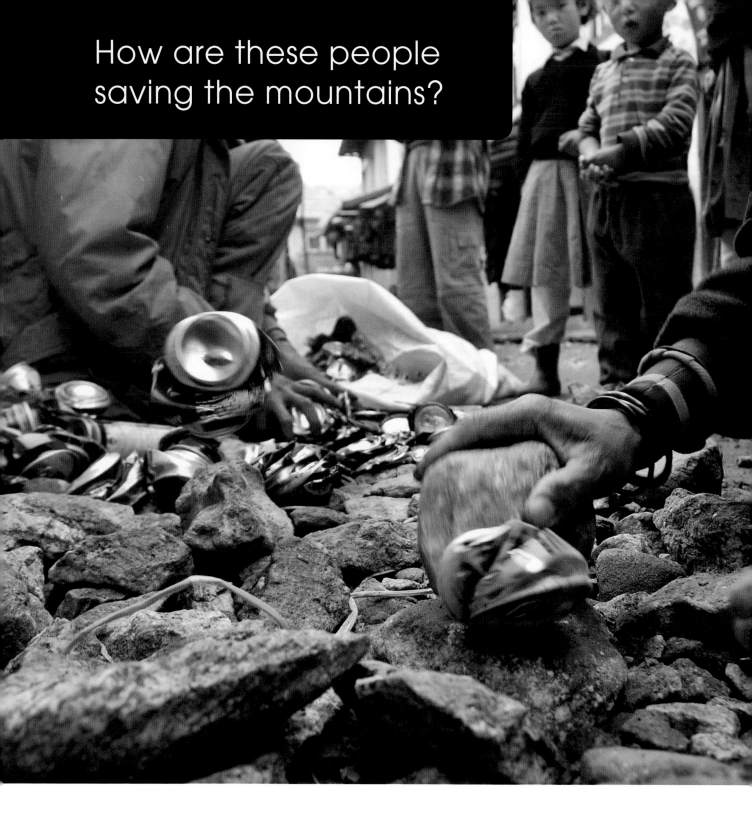

How are these people saving the mountains?

Many people love the mountains and want to visit them. But we have to learn to enjoy the beautiful mountain **environment** without spoiling it. Groups of **mountaineers** have led the way. Some now visit mountains such as Everest with the aim of clearing up the rubbish that has been left there. These volunteers are crushing tins to make them easier to carry away from the Everest trail. Many tonnes of rubbish have been removed.

How can cycling help save the mountains? It may seem strange, but travelling by bike instead of car does help the mountain environment.

Pollution from cars is one of the main causes of **global warming**. Global warming is causing changes in the mountains, as ice melts. This also affects animals and plants that are **adapted** to the original temperature and weather. By fighting global warming, we can help save mountain **habitats**.

WHAT DID YOU FIND OUT ABOUT MOUNTAINS?

What is it that makes the mountain environment unique?
Hint: look at the photographs throughout the book and note down all the different types of landforms and plants that you see. Can you think of any other **environment** where so many features are packed so tightly together? You could also think about how long mountains have stood on Earth.

How has the way humans use mountains changed?
Tip: the photographs on pages 8–9, 10–11, and 14–15 will give you some ideas.

Are there more humans in the mountains today than in the past?
Hint: look at pages 7, 9, 11, and 17 to get some idea of the answer. Once you have an answer, try to work out the different reasons for the change.

How do human leisure activities affect the mountains?
Tip: have a look at the photographs on pages 9, 11, 12, 13, and 27 for some ideas. Split your answers into good effects and bad effects.

Are mountains always safe places? Why is this?
Hint: think about whether mountains are always safe places to have fun, and to live on. The photograph on page 23 might be a good starting point.

How is the climate changing mountains?
Tip: begin your investigation on pages 21 and 22. There are other photographs in the book that show the links between the **climate** and the mountain environment.

How is climate change affecting mountain plants and animals?
Hint: think of ways that mountain plants and animals, including any you can see throughout the book, are specially **adapted** to their environment. If the environment suddenly changes, will they be able to cope?

Even when we are far from the mountains, do our actions affect them?
Tip: look at the photographs on pages 15 and 21 for some ideas about the possible answer to this question.

What are some ways you can help save the mountain environment?
Hint: some of these might not be obvious. When you have your answers to the question above, you might decide there are things you can do far from the mountains that would help them to survive as they are.

Glossary

adapt how a plant or animal changes over time to survive in their habitat

avalanche slide of snow down a mountainside, carrying tonnes of snow, rocks, earth, and trees away with it

border place where two countries meet

building land land on which it is possible to build. Most mountain slopes are too steep to build on, so building land in the flat valley bottoms can be very valuable.

citizen person who belongs to a country or place. Someone who lives near Snowdon in Wales, for example, is a British citizen.

climate average weather and temperature for a particular place. Deserts usually have a hot climate, for example. Mountains are unusual because the climate changes as you climb higher.

dammed closed off or blocked. Rivers are sometimes dammed by nature, for example when beavers deliberately dam the water. Most dams are built by humans.

deforestation removal of trees. Deforestation clears land of all the trees that once grew there.

environment landscape, soil, weather, plants, and animals that together make one place different from another

glacier slow-moving "river" of ice that flows down from a mountain top or ice cap

global warming slow rise in Earth's average temperature. Recent global warming has been caused mainly by human activity.

habitat local environment, which is home to particular kinds of plants and animals

hydroelectric using the power of moving water to make electricity. Hydroelectricity is renewable energy, which is always available and does not cause pollution.

industry business or activity that produces goods for sale

logging cutting down trees to sell or use the wood

mountaineer person who climbs mountains for fun

peak tip of a mountain

piste snowy route down a mountain, specially designed for snowboarders and skiers to use

pollution dirt that harms the environment

rare unusual, not found very often

settlement place where people live close to one another in a community

unique found only in one particular place

valley floor flat area of land at the bottom of a valley

Find out more

Books

Hillary and Norgay's Mount Everest Adventure, Jim Kerr
    (Heinemann Library, 2008)

Landscapes and People: Earth's Changing Mountains, Neil Morris
    (Raintree, 2004)

Mapping Earthforms: Mountains, Catherine Chambers and Nicholas Lapthorn
    (Heinemann Library, 2007)

Mountain Explorer, Greg Pyers (Raintree, 2005)

DVDs

The first **mountaineering** film showed the climb of Mont Blanc, Europe's
highest **peak**, by Frank Ormiston-Smith. It was released in 1903. Ever since,
there have been films about, or set in, the mountains:

Heidi (1937)
This is the story of a girl who lived with her grandfather in a mountain village.
The film gives an idea of how mountain people lived many years ago.

Touching the Void (2003)
The gripping account of British climber Joe Simpson's attempt to save himself
after a fall left him stranded high on a mountain with a broken leg.

Websites
www.mountain.org/education/explore.htm

Explore Mountains can tell you all about how mountains are made, about the
people who live there, and lots of other mountain facts.

www.panda.org/news_facts/education/middle_school/habitats/mountains

This web page from the World Wide Fund for Nature provides information
about mountain **environments**.

Index